Changing the Image of God

From Human to Energy

for dear, wonderful Mary. with love and precious memories Margo

Margo E. Fish

Tapawingo Press
2017

Copyright 2017 by Margo E. Fish

First Printing: 2017

Front and Back Cover Art by Margo Fish

ISBN #: 978-1-387-19911-2

Tapawingo Press
65 Camp Way
PO Box 502
Lake Placid, NY 12946

Acknowledgements

Many friends and family members gave me tender support and understanding. Without them my thesis, now a book, could not have been completed. Libraries and their staff gave me kind assistance. I would like to acknowledge them. Gratitude is lost without a form of expression.

My husband, the late Reverend Doctor Howard M. Fish, was a sustaining support. Our theological discussions allowed ideas to develop. His patience with my isolation while I did my research and writing gave me needed freedom. My children and grandchildren gave compassionate understanding to my days of concentration. Princeton University Libraries and the Princeton Seminary Library provided the opportunity for me to find excellent source materials.

Professor Janet Walton has been a strong and loving advisor. Her guidance and insight sustained me through the writing of my thesis. It was Professor Walton and Professor Williams who advised me to consider the turning the thesis into a published book. I deeply thank her and Dean Hayes and Phillip Paris and Troy Messinger. The students and faculty at Union Theological Seminary gave encouragement and understanding in an atmosphere where learning and unconditional love meet. Many thanks to Kelly Sheehan for her patience and support in the final editing of the manuscript and to Charles Watts who assisted in the editing and publishing of this book. With deepest appreciation I give these words, this book.

Table of Contents

PREAMBLE

It seems appropriate to quote Karen Armstrong: "We need to recover a sense of the importance of the creative imagination in religious quest" and from Emily Dickinson's imagination, when she suggests, "God as poetic process."

This book is about the outworn human image of God and the critical implications that are perpetrated from that image. Art entwines the writing with the threads of theological scholarship along with historical knowledge.

This short book grew from my thesis, written for my degree at Union Theological Seminary in New York City. My advisers urged me to publish it in book form. The thesis was accompanied by an exhibition of my paintings. So with apologies to time and with respect to wonder and imagination and with respects to the recently published books that have emerged on the illusive subject "God", we begin.

For me the subject still remains crucially relevant, with the continued escalation of wars, many related to religions; the hierarchy of controlling powers.

Perhaps a start might be like a round table of wonder, of circular thinking or a sharing, a leaping into the tapestry of doubt, questioning images, and researching into the historical, theological dogmas of religions.

Within this tapestry, at least for Western Cultures and Christians, the image of God is stringently imprinted on our minds, from the earliest arts; Egyptian, Greek, Medieval, into and beyond the potent majesty of Michelangelo's Sistine ceiling image of God as human male.

To create a book metaphorically leaping into religion's myths and into the understanding of art is to accept that the poetic imagination is more comfortable in the ambiguity of understanding than in the pitiable simplistic absolutes.

In sharing my thesis with artists, scholars, and friends, questions or discussions would frequently surface. How does one explain existence and define origin as energy? How do we convey or give meaning to a concept, when the meaning is finally abstract and ambiguous? Can comprehension remain a quest not dwindling to a frozen pragmatism of conclusive definitions?

Ultimately, art has no defining definitions. Religions attempt to define meaning, but the ultimate unknown resists confined definition.

Religions have formalized into institutional organizations. Is it human nature to find comfort in some ritualized knowing? It is obvious that the continued authority of most religions depends upon a comprehensible identity to a God?

Perhaps Goethe, telling of a Greek nobleman who was asked about the education of his children, gives an answer appropriate to this book. The Greek said, "Let them be instructed in that which they will never be able to learn."

Imagination dances toward the passion of understanding, but is restless if caught in the prison of certainty.

Why have we, especially in the western

2

world, created an image of the beginning of the universe as a human, more specifically a male, a "God?"

Questioning the image of God has the possibility of displacing a hierarchical model, an elevated concept of the human society.

Does changing or at least changing the imagining of the Father-God image, to be energy, undo the tradition of a church, synagogue, a temple, a religion, or a person's faith? When people speak about the "God" within - without - what or who is this God?

Is it personal, that is, some form of life that is an all knowing presence? When the word faith is used is that word associated with an image? Does a leap of faith become an abstract spirit of a form? If the image of a religion's God exists, its image affects societies. Do we transcend systems, that is, the orthodox of institutions, by changing the image?

This book, this theological journey, this inquiry, becomes the process for the leap of the imagination, not a dogma, not a thesis or a religious substitute, but a quest like a Holy Grail - Where is the Holy Grail? - where the questioning sustained the earth. Assumptions can preemptively become dogmas, corner stones for the castles of authority.

Restructuring, like the grains of sand, move the stones into the movable imagination's microbes of a constant new seeing.

Art can become an initiative form, an image, but simultaneously into the paradox of process. With apologies to words, that might become a paralysis of thoughts or stagnant in their attempt for meaning. We begin or continue with a very young history, relative to origin, if there were an origin. Is there a before time? Theories of evolution - relativity - are like the threads bearing the wonder of origin, of existence. Even the moon is evolving.

Any historical period of observation is limited to the exposure of the wisdom available.

If the image of God (human) has inflicted us with an arrogance of reasoning, can any human untangle the web of its inheritance?

Imagination with discipline is one of the basic tools for an artist. The exploration of thought can become the naked gift of a possible transcendence beyond the limitation of national boundaries, dogmas, obsolescent concepts.

Whether religious insight breeds forgiveness, compassion, love, and openness to an educated restless curiosity or to monotheism of absolutes is quintessential to be asked.

The educated questioning does not necessarily lead to alienation or a faithless society, but perhaps toward prophetic understanding.

Can the arts, or do the arts, create a temple of wonder, a garden for a global theater of shared Grace?

A parallel hovers with this quest; when the absence of absolutes could possibly lead to, for example the obsolescence of war, to a healing of the earth, to an ecological global identity.

A technological vineyard of webbing vines,

we realize, accompanies this quest. As our complex beautiful universe continues to unfold its immensity it becomes even greater with the gifts of research from scientific minds, including potent visual imprint from the media - film, television, websites, video games - is an obvious invasion of the image of the universe, perhaps requiring another manuscript. However, the quest, the changing image of God, to energy, within a contemporary culture does remain.

So on to this brief book; for pleasure, passion, and into gentle doubts, and a questioning quest.

> "To see the world in a grain of sand
> And Heaven in a wild flower
> Hold infinity in the palm of one's hand
> And eternity in an hour."
>
> William Blake

OVERTURE

In the beginning was the image, the silent image,
the sacred poetry of the soul.

"We do not use symbols we are symbols. These
images create us no less than we create them.
Change our images and we change not only reality
but ourselves." [1]

Thomas Ketling

To probe and ramble into metaphysics, to dare to enter into the depth of the meaning of art and religion, is to enter into the primordial unity of origin. It is to wander into the ultimate essence of creation itself and participate in the ontological meaning of existence. It is to acquire some means of comprehending a universal insight of art and religion without the orthodoxy of definition.

Proust wandered into this dilemma when he said, "Creative arts originate, in fact, not from knowledge of their laws, but from an incomprehensible and obscure power that is not fortified by being explained." [2]

The great question of how images have affected religions, and in turn, us, is not answerable. It is not answerable, for it reaches into the ultimate questions of being, of art and religions.

Image transcends the vocabulary of words. As an expression of faith, image is categorically subjective and resists dogmatic theocratic reasoning. [3]

To dare to enter the world of religions is to join the same chorus and question the reasons for origin itself and all the supplemental words ordained by religious authorities.

A thesis or any writing ultimately requires the boundaries of limitation, but to limit our imagination to pages of linear writing is not to see Rembrandt at his altar of fire, is not to see some fierce burning of his soul, that gave his palette freedom to portray the human species addressing themselves to the heavens and crying in the wilderness to the 'Holy Why'.

If the artist, as Redon felt, "comes to life for a fulfillment which is mysterious and the meaning of mystery is always to be in ambiguity" [4], the template of our seeing is in ambiguity. It is in the arms of mystery. The quest to comprehend this mystery (the blueprint, the images of our civilization) must therefore be involved with ultimate ontological questions.

The questions about artists as interpreters of religious insights accompanies the quest. Where does the source of this 'fulfillment' have its guidance?

We word our religions but the image becomes the profound stability of those words. It is a portraiture of the mystery and remains a potent inscription upon the human, society, and now, of course, in the complexity of internet global technology.

"The last word on art should indeed be mystery". [5]

"The experience of great art disturbs one like a deep anxiety for another, like a near-escape from death, like a long anesthesia for surgery: it is a massive blow from which one recovers slowly and which leaves one changed in ways that only gradually come to light" [6]

Jacques Barzun

"The deep shock of apprehending a great work of art is no affectation. Something takes place and it is tremendous." [7]

E. M. Forster supports this enormous strength when saying, "Every artist on the contrary professes to create a world more real and solid than daily existence [a world] eternal and indestructible." [8]

The power of art [imaged] and the phenomenon of mystery is the conception of Margaret Miles, who believed when art is viewed as the primary language for the expression of faith, it assumes an importance that transcends modern aesthetic criteria. [9]

"These words of religion and art are paradoxically parallel and intersect only at infinity." (Quote from Mircea Eliade) [10]

Part of the parallel is in the vein of this ontological potency of source [origin] and succumbs to the arena of the numinous.

"Before religion became morality with emotion it was emotion itself, or a group of emotions, and it still is. Those emotions are, the feeling of the uncanny, the thrill of awe or reverence, the sense of dependence, impotency, or of nothingness or of religious rapture and exultation. They are the non-rational feelings, the sense of the tremendous, the awful, the mysterious, or numinous." [11]

The numinous is a dialectical affair in which the yes becomes a no and the no becomes a yes and art is a dialectical affair. [12]

These emotions are part of the basis of Paul Tillich's theology, he drawing them from Schelling. "Outside of that which pure thought discovers as being in the state or possibility, there exists a reality external to thought." [13]

In art, George Heyer acknowledges a similar concept, "What the artist creates is more than the sum of its parts." [14]

Carrying the numinous even further Paul Tillich links the theological quest to art, "Art is an expression of ultimate concern." [15]

At another time when he was dedicating a house in Potsdam, this connecting tissue between religion and art continued. He formed this holy paradoxical relationship in words. The meaning moves to mystery when he said, "Art presents the tension between finite and infinite space. The beholder encounters a limited form which is pregnant with meaning." [16]

It seems appropriate to take Tillich's statement and ask the question, is ultimate concern of humanity an expression of the artist? The more haunting question, of course is where is the source of ultimate reality? If the artist is attempting to express some primordial reality that is finally undefinable and mysterious. Is it contaminated always by culture and the religion of its time?

Kant's theory of aesthetics compliments the importance and complexity of art. To explore the meaning of art is inherent to the human consciousness, to explain it, returns us to the numinous. He describes the limits of rationally where there is a pondering that is deeply meaningful, but at the same time incapable of "complete translation into intellectual propositions and concepts." [17]

In Plato's dialogue Phaedo, the most penetrating thoughts out of necessity take the form of the figurative. [18]

As an artist, I stumble about in paint and canvas conversing with these thoughts, about origin, about the artist, and the dangers of an inauthentic connection pertaining to the translation of an inner hearing to an outer doing. I am in that shadow of William Blake,
when he asked the rhetorical question, "Do you 'Sir' paint with fear and trembling?" [19]

This mystery, this ultimate reality and its image, is a consuming quest. It has been the sacred focus of my years at Union Theological Seminary. It motivates a search into the writings of the physicists, into the work of Jung, and the primary connection to a universal. It is to ask why the human gave this wholly other, this categorical imperative, this Yahweh, a human form and if that form is a constituent of the ultimate mystery?

Where does it belong? Is it the tragic flaw?

The image is in the glue of theology. It sticks to the language and does not stay on the Sistine Chapel, but fortifies a grandeur of the human in spite of the feminists calling, in spite of the 'Grace' emerging from the quantum physicists and biologists, such as Lynn Margules.

By Grace I mean some insight, some gift that converses with the holy why within our beings and frees it from a pathology of inherited dogma into a sacred rhythm of the universe.

When the physicists such as Geoffrey Chew writes (or Fritjof Capra), the pedestal of hierarchy is removed and we fall into the embrace of comprehensive wonder of living particles. We are participants in a biological interconnecting God.

Ecological awareness will arise when we combine our rational knowledge with an intuition for the non-linear nature of our environment. The search into mythologies releases the anthropomorphic static insight of comprehending the universe. [20]

Chew's bootstrap theory moves our image, our God, our theology, our art. His comprehensive theory of subatomic particles not only abandons the idea of fundamental building blocks of matter, but accepts no fundamental entities whatsoever – no fundamental constants – laws or equations. The universe is seen as a dynamic web of interrelated events. [21]

To elaborate further either on the quantum physics or to begin to probe systematically the writings of the feminist theology is not possible here. It is possible, through these suggestions, to let the rivers of insight deepen.

This book is not an historical account of art history, nor an analysis of Christian art in particular. Corby Finney in his book, <u>Invisible God</u>, has written a thorough and detailed study of early Christian art. [22] It documents in careful detail what I can only hint upon. This book is not an analysis of particular works of art nor a proof for or against the existence of God. It is about the image of God. Yet I will concentrate on a few artists for some grounding of the power of image. Briefly I will trace our roots in the western tradition. To separate influence categorically is impossible. The complexity of the subject intensifies the importance. Clarity emerges in our awareness that comprehending is in the incomprehensible.

We are washed in a collective artistic and intellectual ocean. Our waters are Greek, Roman, European, Scientific, Celtic, all orthodoxies, neo orthodoxies, primitive, Christian, Jewish, Hindu and nature herself. To name all is to inhabit time itself. We share the catacombs of each other's souls.

We are the particle of the sacred universe and heirs to the mysterium. Art is an associate of theology and a religious quest. Is there an 'a priori' to the human consciousness that graces our understanding and its expressions?

This book might be described as a journey through invisible archetypes that are intrinsically formless but become visible art. The archetypes, in turn are the driving implications of creation. Creation is the process of ultimate reality. Can we dare to make static the image of this moving mystery, knowing the power of images, and still remain in the wisdom T.S. Elliot posed as the only one, the wisdom of humility? [23] Would we ask these questions if they were not already seeded in us?

The rhetorical questions are the rivers for thought and continue in an ambiguous flow. Is it possible to move cultures from a God as creator to Gaia as process through the strength of image? This is a critical question when our earth is stagnating from the human ascension enthroned from an image of the patriarchal builder, God. Is art an escape from the final seal of our finitude?

Trusting David Martin's statement in his book, Art And The Religious Experience is to become a participator in the receptive creativity of the artist. It is also, he writes, to trust that the art has an ontological sensitivity that is 'more adequate than the non-artist." "The artist focuses to a fine point that aboriginal light of Being, present to us all but usually concealed or confused that illuminates our societies, our world. Insofar as our ontological sensitivities are enlightened, we are saved from 'ontical slavery'."[24] By understanding our ontical slavery we can more easily move toward a freedom from it.

If religion is about wholeness, what is the appropriate structure of wholeness for our times? What are our new images of God?

Father Thomas Berry, the author of the

prophetic book, <u>The Story of the Universe</u> said in a lecture, "I do not use the word God now, it is too loaded." [25]

Our traditional image of God stagnates us in one we have out grown. What is the artist perceiving? Our present soul landscape appears barren in this culture of popularized media images.

We cannot live with a traditional image of God and it seems we cannot live without some answer to this forming universe. Like a search for the Holy Grail, the artist, all humanity, freed from dogma, can listen to the heartbeat of a universe, now understood as dancing molecules, always in process.

Understanding requires the views perceived through time. The image of God, the image of 'the wholly other' belongs to a family in that time. Tracing this visible conception [image making and the image makers of our religious landscape] is an invitation into some majesty, into humanity's awakening the portrayal of the everlasting mystery of creation into religion itself.

FIRST MOVEMENT

"The logos is more readily perceived by the eye
than by the ear." [26]

In the beginning was God.

The Legacy of Image.

Image emerges out of our records of the
universe as insightful, controversial, profound
mystical, threatening, healing, grounding and
transformative. The depths of its sources can be
studied to the degree that any intention can be
discerned, and that is often hypothesis, but never
less than creation forming itself. We can perceive
the meaning of images in time from the comments
written at the time. Retrospection never separates
itself from the bias of time. Our penetration is
inference. The archaeological symbols lie in
silence. Their contemporary viewers, the ones
who saw the images, are silent. The writers who
wrote about the images are few and they were the
authorities in positions of authority in their time.
Positioned authorities are most often concerned
with control and control is not art. To trace the
history of image is to invite the legacy of image to
our table and there in its great array recognize its
immutable   presence   and   sustaining   and
penetrating communion.
    The hand of God in the hand of the artist
has already bestowed an irrepressible question.
What and where are the sources of the images?

"Seeing comes before words, the child looks and recognizes before it can speak." [27]

Yet the paradox: the Bible dangles before us another legacy and we read, "In the beginning was the word and the word was with our God." [John 1:1]

It is seeing which grounds our place in our visible world. We do give explanation to that world in words, but words cannot undo our awareness that we are in the midst of this Holy earth – universe.

Magritte, the artist, wrote about the gap between words and what we see or are seeing. The painting concerning this was The Key of Dreams. "The sun setting never quite appropriates the words of the scientist that the earth is simply turning away from the sun." [28]

Written history is rightly so, worded history. The Greeks, Jews and Christians write the records of humanity's dialogue with some 'wholly other'. From the beginning of human life to its end this dialogue continues.

"Though it does indeed sound
dangerous, it is in no way
reprehensible to say that every
'man' creates a God for himself nay,
must make himself such a God, in
order to honor in him the one who
created him." [29]

A descriptive hierarchy of the God emerges and languishes in the 'heavens'; loving, creating, casting rods in and out conversing with the infinite and minuteness of the souls – minds imagination (in our history).

Before we search through image, John Berger, in <u>Ways of Seeing</u>, suggests a few definitions of image, though definitions do not define, and art does not rest in defining. Our culture sits like a vulture wanting to solve problems and problems solvers want definitions.

Even Berger's definitions of images wring the meaning out of art. We are left with a wet cloth, deprived, and unidentifiable.

> He says, "An image is a sight which has been recreated or reproduced. It is an appearance or a set of appearances, which has been detached from the place and time in which it first made its appearance and preserved for a few moments or a few centuries. Every image embodies a way of seeing. "Images", he continues, "were first made to conjure up the appearances of something that was absent. Gradually it became evident it could outlast what it represented." [30]

The four major cradle lands of civilization, Mesopotamia, Egypt, India and China, enter history with a single, supreme God, dwelling in the sky. [31] The power of patriarchy has been extremely difficult to understand because it is all pervasive. It has influenced our most basic ideas about human nature and our relation to the universe. [32]

> "Hindu and Christian Titanism meet in Raimon Panikkar, who suggests that man is in some ways the successor of God, the agent of divinity, the destiny of God is in man's power, in so much as man is, God is not, in so far as God is, man is not, the one means the absence of the other." [33]

Panikkar says this view leads to an "all embracing cosmotheandric reality." But it is thoroughly Titanism [God] centered and the cosmos collapses into the human form.

Titan comes from a name for older Gods who under Prometheus stormed Mt. Olympus and raged against Zeus and other Olympian deities for the control of the Universe. [34]

Religions that put humans first, Western or Eastern emerge in a period now named the axial period. Western people discovered and responded to human individually by externalizing their desires. [35] Indians – East turned inward in an awareness of this self-world view (self-God). Their prototype for the world has human characteristics. The Jains, to be saved, have for their focus of spiritual liberation a God who eventually has a human incarnation. [36]

Whether our present analysis of early art is true will only be known when and if knowing is ever possible. To search, to untangle the self-world God image and its earliest roots is to discern somehow the conscious and preconscious patterns in our earliest cultures.

The earliest Ice Age naturalist's paintings of animals are symbols. Erich Neumann believes that they were the actual essence of the animal species. The bison is a spiritual poacher symbol. The drawing or painting actually encompasses the numinous heart or the center of the animal's living world. It is the spirit itself. There is no self-world of separation. The forms of the archetypal elements of the culture have an unconscious understanding. This is now called period of origination. [37]

The pole, for the Arunta tribe, (the Achilpa) in mythical times, fashioned from the trunk of a gum tree, is carried with them as they roam. It is the axis mundi, a cosmic axis. By being around this pole it allows them to always be in their world and centered if it is broken it denotes catastrophe. It is a symbol, but is their world not a part from but a part of. [38]

In the axial period a period of systematization of consciousness and the time of a very strong emergence of the individual ego, a collective consciousness arises. It is in each culture with definite archetypes and becomes a dogmatic heritage of a group.

The unknown powers of the actual symbol are separate from the person. The person giving it form is adorned in the axial period. It is the percolation of an image where the group celebrating it are individuals casting a projection. With the growth of individuality, the integral situation of the creative element in oneness of the group disintegrates. The response is a receptive relationship. [39]

This receptive relationship, ornament as ornament, did not fit into the unity of life in primitive art and the art of classical antiquity.

The ornament had actual meaning. Our decorations are ornaments. If we have lion claws on our chairs it is ornamental. For the Egyptian the lion claw on a sofa meant resting on a lion itself, who was the sun God and who overcomes death. Rest there was a prelude to eternal life.

Every line and circle in early Greek painting (geometric period) had its own meaning. The religious purpose of the vases is not conditioned by its subject. The subject or symbol is the object. [40]

Drawing in perspective gave evidence to how the human was situated in the world. One was no longer a component among all others but rather is a separate "ego" freed from it. Greek philosophy made this view of the world possible.

The world becomes something other than this world; it becomes another world. Therefore the image is not the actual energy portrayed, but what one knows apart from this world. The form derives meaning in the way it is created. Power is imaged it is not power itself.

The image of God, the portraiture of the divine, unequivocally becomes the projected image of the power made human in the guise of the wholly other, the God.

The initial strength of an image which pre-egocentric cultures experienced, justified the fear that the emerging Judaism and Islamic and Christian religions associated with a "primitive magic". [41]

Once God was represented as man, not animal or inanimate object, the "magic" now lost from association of the symbol both caused suspicion and regret. Fear of the magic restrained the image. Imagination was passed into categorical poverty in art.

Plato makes the poet (arts) responsible for evil (magic). They had to represent divinity. Human forms lacked the ideal. Art had to be ideal.

Homer created the half divine, half human being. Later in the Old Testament, the writers choreographed the dilemma. The image of 'man', in the concept of God, had to be corrected. "God repents, no he is not a 'man', so he could repent nothing. Satan, not God tempts David." [42]

The code for the image of western God emerges as human and male, apart from 'wholly other'.

> And God said, "Let us make man in
> our image in the image of God so
> God created man in his own image,
> of God. He created he him, male
> and female created he them."
> [Genesis I:26-27]

The Phoenix bird, a pre-Christian image for renewal of life, becomes Christ's resurrection. The orant or orans becomes a Christian praying for departed souls. The four horses of Phaeton becomes Elijah being taken into heaven. [43]

Cassier, in his book <u>The Philosophy of Symbolic Forms</u>, found through his research, that man can apprehend and know his own being only in so far as he can make it visible in the image of his Gods. Just as he learns to understand the structure of this body and limbs only by becoming a creator of tools and products, so he draws from his spiritual creations – language, myth and art. He seems to comprehend himself as an independent cosmos with its own peculiar 'laws'. [44]

The power of art the visible, the eventual casting of form, this desire to see, to fasten identify of the God or its perception penetrates our existence.

Early Christians were influenced by ancient concepts: that humans could not have a direct picture of God, and that if they did see God, they could not represent what they saw.

This ancient concept is likely to be the one inherited from the Greeks, where, using one example, Euripides (Bacchae 7) tells of the warning that Dionysus's human mother must never see Zeus in his true form. It evolves into averting our eyes and not to create, if we did see, the image of Yahweh. God was absolute power, to dispel that power into form was a sacred taboo. [45] "Thou shalt have no graven image." [Exodus 20:4-5]

In the 6th century B.C., in the pre Socratic era, the divinity was not describable. It was of abstract qualities. This in turn led, centuries later, to a negative theological paradigm. This God cannot be known or seen, or defined. This seems to have roots in Democritus's concept of the universe that the world evolved naturally from the chance combinations of atoms that existed eternally. [46]

Though history reads that the image of God was forbidden, archaeology contradicts this belief.

Image was alive and vital. Why in the spite of certain intellectual decrees does art emerge like a constant ocean tide? Why has the artist (the more ontologically sensitive) divined the Gods apart from this universe and human (and we add male)? Is an artist only guided by a culture or are artists capable of seeing some buried archetype knowing? The tides of possibilities search our shores – our souls.

The catacombs are testamental pictured symbolism, the legacy of art contradicts the legacy of word. When art was allowed in the church (Constantine Era) its purpose was not solely for the non-literate.

Margaret Miles, in her research, concludes in her book, Image as Insight, that art was one of a communal event, a sacred creative event. It was not for the purpose to instruct the non-literate. [47]

Corby Finney says, in his book Invisible God, the concept of art for the illiterate came from much later interpreters. The Byzantines and reformation polemicists had relegated art to an inferior expression. [48]

Plato had banished artists from his republic. They were a luxury and not affordable. There was the fear of the demonic power that arose from the artists. The real could possess the demonic. However once the ideal was allowed to be portrayed in the republic the ideal created the vision. The vision emerged as a meditative instrument, a transforming expression toward an ideal. Later the medieval ages initiated this form of art when the body the sacred, the Godliness is experienced through the image.

Plotinus interpreting Plato in the third century helps to strengthen the mediating use of image. Objects are to be left behind. They are not a step toward knowledge, but a mirror to catch the image of the 'All'. One is to concentrate on the mediating function of images. [49]

Clement (3rd century), the apologist, applies Platonic doctrine of representative to fraud and the eighth commandment against theft. The sculptor and painter copy and mimic nature: it is robbery. It belongs to the lower world. Truth belongs to the upper world (Noetic realm).

Alexandrians give art a message; art purporting to represent divinity can only reproduce the world of appearance, illusions and deceptions. It distorts truth therefore it is evil. [50]

In later centuries we hear an echo with Martin Luther's saying, "The ears are the only organs of a Christian, not the eyes". [51]

The stern warning seems to have had antiquity in mind, picturing Pygmalion in his creating such convincing and supreme sculptures he becomes so frustrated he succumbs to wanting to make love to a piece of stone. [52] There is new argument abroad concerning the accepted views coming from the apologists. It appears Christians would not be seduced with the rhetoric of the Alexandrians.

Sister Charles Murray published a brief article read by Margaret Miles that challenged the consensus held so long by the scholastic tradition. [53]

"No protagonist of the hostility
theory has yet been able to produce

one single clear statement from any Christian writer which says that non-idolations artistic representation is wrong." [54]

It is not possible in this book to discuss the lengthy work concerning the early apologist' writings. I can only suggest that the present analysis of the forced explanation on the value of image was indeed forced. No fourth century author felt they had to make an argument against art. Pope Gregory I defense of the inspirational value of art was written a century later.

"Fourth century rationales for religious images are few, brief, and unsystematic. The role of religious images was seldom questioned and therefore did not need systematic defense." [55]

Corby Finney continues to substantiate Sister Murray's writings. The apologists' attacks on art were apologetic conceits. They wrote in exaggerations to defend the new church by extreme rage against the "pagan world" who lacked "the most elementary ideas of God and how God should be worshiped." [56]

The Christians' attitude in question during the second and third centuries certainly reflected the antagonistic repulsion against the images of the Roman Empire. The forced role of an imperial image would have caused resentment and been a persuasive consensus to negate certain forms of image. Pliny's introduction of the imperial image into the courtroom had severe consequences. It intensified Rome as a persecutor of early Christians. [57]

To leave this contention to the scholars of that period is necessary, but not to leave the historical evidence of the symbolic pictorial language on the walls of underground tombs and the generic figures, shepherds, philosophers, magicians, and fishermen. Did Pliny drive the nail into the coffin of pictorial tradition as Corby Finney suggests, giving reason for the lack of portraits of Mary or Jesus or Paul or Peter? [58]

We know that art costs money. Other worldliness or anti-materialism in Christianity's earliest years would also deter the arts. Later, monetary support ushers in the support of the arts.

It is the liberating influence of the Constantinians as well as the substantial support of the church that allows the stilled tradition of non-generic figures to again be created.

The significance of image is within the very profound essence of our existence. It shapes, confounds, and creates a religious attitude. It is our soul's companion. It is not an orphan and an elevated separated portraiture. It is the figurative essence of the 'wholly other', the creator.

The medieval arts in churches became the significant aspect of the worship itself. Vision was the access of the object and the object image increased piety and love. [59]

The actual touching of the Christ through the worshiper's visual ray, was salvific. Viewing the consecrated bread was equal to, if not more intense that, ingesting the bread. [60]

Roger Bacon attempted to scientifically prove that not only the viewer but the object itself had energy rays. [61]

Late medieval visual liturgy was an experience of the visual and minimally of the word.

The Protestant reformation retrieved the word. Meister Eckhart documents the blessedness of the 'heaven', it being a passive activity. Art is again moved into the legacy of a separated element, a lessor code for the mystery of God. Calvin, Zwingli, and Luther among a few, marginalized art for the reformation. Religious education made the 'Word' become again sacred and dominate. [62]

Our understanding of that form of pietism from a distance, however, needs the soundings from the accompaniment of the authoritative presence of the Last Judgment.

The fear of the holocaust of hell wrapped in the theological equivalent of image, a negative ingredient solution brought down the arts. The word created for educated and lay energized the removal of the iconoclastic image.

It was not because the image was weak, or not adored, but because it was too strong and loved.

Luther did remark that he still pictured Christ hanging from a cross the way he saw his own image in the reflection of waters, in spite of the pronouncement about image. [63]

"The image is the principle of our knowledge. It is that from which

29

our intellectual activity begins, not as a passing stimulus, but as an enduring foundation. When the imagination is choked so also is our theological knowledge." [64]

This connection is made by Hans Kung in his conception of painting. He elevates the artist as Romano Guardini claims that "art functions eschatologically". The tree is painted beautifully so that the tree beautifully painted on canvas is not sealed in its unreality, but raises the hope in short for a new heaven and a new earth." [65]

The real human being is not what he is, and as he is, but what he essentially is. The real transition should be one from existence to essence. The symbolism in the image reads then as, Being as transcendental. [66]

This transcendental quality seems to be what Tillich meant in his Museum and of Modern Art lecture. He said after visiting Botticelli Madonna and Child with singing angels:

"I felt a state approaching ecstasy. In the beauty of the painting there was beauty itself. It shines through the colors of the paint as the light of day shines through the stained glass windows of a medieval church." [67] "As I stood there bathed in the beauty I turned away shaken." Later he wrote, "That moment has affected my whole life, given me

the keys of the interpretation of
human existence brought vital joy
and spiritual truth." [68]

Art – image is in the marrow of our
understanding of religion, ourselves, our universe.

Religions' comprehension of itself is proudly in
the world of image. Its significance in and out of the
church is an encounter with the universe. Theology is
bereft without it, and paradoxically, confined if the
image is seen without understanding the historical
perspective.

Art is banished by the church then accepted. It
confounds the philosopher, the theologians, the artist.
What now are all our confoundments in this precious
world?

From Plato to Plotinus, to the writings of
Margaret Miles, in Paul Tillich's: theology, from the
earliest being to those presently living, the image –
art engages the soul and imprints and thrusts life into
a revelation, revealing the silence of the mystery we
have named God.

One of the strongest images of God is
Michelangelo's Sistine Ceiling image of God creating
Adam. His noble genius has infected universally our
imaginations.

It has radiated an authority. To enter or at least
explore his religious world is like entering the moon
in order to comprehend and more fully live in its
light. We cannot, but we can imagine. The radiance is
there, its source belongs to the ontology of existence.

SECOND MOVEMENT

Michelangelo, the portraiture of God.

Artists engraving the image.

All art is concerned with "penetrating into the heart of life." [69]

Horace said, in his <u>Art of Poetry</u>, "The mind is more slowly stirred by the ear then by the eye." [70]

"Translate verbal messages into visual form if you want to remember." [71]

The father, human image of God remains in the tabernacle of the imagination. My childhood picture-filled Bible shapes the word God and though theologically, spiritually and intellectually I do not perceive 'the wholly other', the ultimate reality, as human or male, the image of art history's heritage, the museums, books, are indelibly placed, like an attic trunk, in this soul's being.

Susanne Langer discusses this initial education by the arts with which we live. We are, she believed, formulated by the picture books we looked at, by the images we see frequently, by the music we hear. The art forms our daily life. [72]

I have asked friends over the years what their image of God is. Most recently our granddaughter said, "Air." Professor Ted Gill said, "A yes." A spoken atheist said, "If driven to identify the image for creator God, it would be a butterfly." [73]

The majority remain on the Sistine Chapel image; God, bearded, fathering creation. Though they footnote their answers with a revision, unconscious patterning. The word 'God' is man, white, bearded and old.

Some of the reasons given for art is the suspicion of the human's lack. We are born naked without tusks or claws, cannot run very fast, we have no shell, but we could observe and translate that observation into visual forms. Does art have the germ of that nature, is that lack a transformational need? Does our projected God inherit this suspicion, this lack, or is it a soul's connection to a Holy Mystery?

"Art is better able to convey the
holy then the pure idea for its parts
of departure is the whole man, body
and soul, an invisible unity." [74]

Kierkegaard's phrases this invisible unity as preliminary. Beauty and holiness approach each other, growing distant until finally they in the far distance cannot be held apart. We erect no ultimate truths but remain modestly to one side. Something is noticed dimly. It is a pointing toward. [75]

"For those able to contemplate life
with some measure of detachment
like the poet who sees life steadily
and sees it whole, was
Michelangelo carrying a whole
world within himself." [76]

What is this world, this world of Michelangelo and his God?

From Michelangelo's letters we perceive his God as a doer, a maker, an interloper, a being present who could help and deserved thanksgiving and gratitude. He would be imaged as the great white father, in the heavens.

In the year 1507, January 22nd, from Florence, he wrote to Buonarota Di Lodovico, "That's all", "Pray to God for me that things may go well." [77]

> "I expect to be ready about Lent to cast this figure of mine, so pray to God it may go well for me, because if it goes well, I hope to have the good fortune to be in favor with this Pope." [78]

Another letter again reads like a prayer, this time, not a praying need, but one of thankfulness to God.

> "For your information on Friday afternoon at 2 o'clock Pope Julius came to the premises where I am working and stayed to watch me at work for about half an hour. Then he gave me his blessing and went away. He was evidently pleased with what I am doing. For that I think we must thank God above all and this I beg you to do and pray for me." [79]

Michelangelo's withdrawal from society periodically was for him to turn to himself unable to endure the "exquisite agony" of estiemo ardore. He cried unto the God of love to restore him to himself.

These few letters and biographical comments point the way toward the God figure of Michelangelo's faith.

He became intoxicated with the physical beauty of the human being but even more with the spiritual beauty of the soul as it is communicated through the eyes. [80] "Before men I do not say before God, I count myself an honest man." [81]

In this spirit and salvation of his soul, he devoted the last years of his life to that art which he believed God had assigned to him. [82]

It is impossible to understand completely anyone's deepest inquiry with his/her God. Michelangelo moved over a paradoxical and dialectical terrain. His deeply Christian mind portrayed paradox. In his mind everything generated opposites. In his ironic underlying consciousness. He could be religious and irreligious. Michelangelo participated in the late renaissance discussions. Absorbing Neo-Platonism, reading the writings of Origen, Philo, Basil, Ambrose, Augustine to Mirandola of Michelangelo's time. [83]

The Christian doctrine of Creation was discussed in comparison to the classical cosmogenies. The Neoplatonic was familiar in Renaissance courtly culture. The importance of order, the centrality of quality, was understood as a life principle in opposition to matter. Philosophically, moral concepts involved the self-suppression of the rebellious body though awareness of a beauty which with aspiration becomes less tangible and more spiritual until at last the soul dominates both orally and aesthetically and leads to immortality. [84]

The art that imitates God creates living things and "perfect painting" rather than merely appealing to the senses. Only God and the painter can animate matter, give it life and grace and spirit. [85]

These are strong convictions that implore Michelangelo as they did Dante. The true art imitates the work of God. Not only did the artist like God create ex-nihilo, but his art followed the order of divine creation as "that the invisible things of world are clearly seen being understood by the things that are made." [Romans 1:20]

How were these ideas to be manifested as he pondered a unity for his Sistine visible identity of God? For Michelangelo the vision of the God-like powers of the artist very likely were supported from the writings of Ficino's cosmic vision of homoartifex 'deus in terris'. [86]

The universality of God's creative power is in the artist. The artist had the license for a paradoxical illusion of classical form and sophistic fantastic invention. How difficult to uncover the edict of the artist's primordial relationship to interpretation. Jerome's dismissal of Perseus, seems applicable, "If you do not wish to be misunderstood, I do not wish to understand you" seems applicable. [87]

Michelangelo was less an embodiment of the spirit of his age than he was a genius choosing among and exploring some of the many possibilities that tradition offered him. [88]

This reformation of the artist as prophet moves the artistic freedom into a rising social position.

Michelangelo chose at the end to reject fantasy and turned his understanding to the order of nature forsaking the rational order for the irrational order of revealed truth.

He shifted and probed the stone seeking out its life and grace, impossibly shifting figures in its dense mass one last time trying to make life with his hands.

Was the great father - God - a biographical image? Does the monumental image of God born from the great birthing womb of his philosophical, religious, primordial searching spirit, that shook the foundation of Michelangelo's soul, free us toward the same paradoxical search?

Though he hung God in the tapestry of man, that tapestry must fall from its pinnings, if the fabric of our artistic heritage listens to the orchestrations of the numinous, this cry and laughter of our souls' visitations with the miracle of life, will evolve .

To unpin images seems only possible and plausible by demystifying the image, but paradoxically retaining the inherent mystery.

Sallie McFague, in her book <u>Models Of God</u>, concludes, "that we are individuals not separated from one another, but beings in relationship to a most radical and thoroughgoing nature, not as a machine but an organ internally and externally related." [89] Still, she believes as complex humans we are models for a God.

Art was to be revealed in the residence of an all knowing God.

To remain there is to remain in a Michelangelo separation, a God – an (a priori) a Creator God.

In Richard Niebuhr's theology, which paradoxically says "none is absolute save God and the absolutizing of anything finite is ruinous to the finite itself," [90] God is being examined.

It leads us toward the theology of Gordon Kaufman. Gordon Kaufman's description of God's image was to conceive an image of God that was multifarious, biological that made human existence possible. It was an activity of God intrinsic to an ecological sensitivity of creation. [91]

As far back as Schleiermacher, the thorough going absolutizing of God had begun to fall. But the god remained still, a God-world relationship. Michelangelo's God is there but less visible.

Paul Tillich is shaking the foundations. The God is not falling from Grace, but Grace is calling upon the absolute.

In The Theological Imagination, Kaufman says, "the central task of theologians in every culture is to work out, to construct an image/concept of God appropriate to contemporary life." [92] "The world of art is the important world for the revelation to place." [93]

Its appropriateness that Kaufman points toward is analogous to the recent book, The Disappearance of God, a Divine Mystery by Richard Friedman. In a brilliant study he traces the disappearance of God through the course of the Hebrew Bible narrative. He reminds us that both Judaism and Christianity developed with a consciousness of "the divine hiddenness." [94]

After centuries of hiddenness in Christianity, God becomes visible again in a human flesh. Christ and the word became flesh and dwelled among us. God is visible. In a bit of irony the "son of man", as Jesus called himself, reunites us with God and we become hidden again. Here ends his book. [95]

Nietzsche's Death of God, in a sense, is a hidden one, is some search for a primal identity that was entertained even in the patriarchal setting of the Old Testament.

Hiding away is another or at least a symbol toward our emerging concept of this universe. Copernicus tormented the religious doctrines of his time. We were but a tiny spectrum of the infinite, not at its center. [96] Now we are a bundle of moving particles. God is the participating microscopic dwelling.

What happens to our moralities, to our insightful religious suspended need for omnipotence in our age of a cosmological Gaian configuration?

The configuration of a spiritual energy is no longer imaged as human, in a opaque costume of hierarchy. It is a relentless motion spirited with atoms and inertia beyond absolutes. The hearings from a big bang experiment done by the physicists: Penzias, Wilson, and Joel Primack, said the vibrations were like the birth of the universe, erratic, but forming. George Smott, who was present to the experiment also said, "If you're religious, it's like looking at God." [97] It is saturated with connected energies.

Celebration and awe can only accompany this participation in our universe. Our intention to love is in the labyrinth of God, now a festival of a Gaian parable, creation itself. It is microscopic mythology of four billion years of microcosms. Our cavalier attitude of human species, no less, a God image is rendered to a spectrum of molecules, no perhaps, rendered to the survival of Planet Earth. [98]

"The physiological system of life on earth, Gaia, could easily survive the loss of humanity, whereas humanity would not survive apart from that life." [99]

The nineteenth century produced a Nietzsche, Death of God, and simultaneously the artists; Redon, Cezanne, Matisse.

The image was running. The physicists were viewing our hermeneutics of physiology and the artists were the interpreters.

The breaking of atoms, of God, the absolute was an essence becoming the canvases of artists.

To move to their image moves us toward Gaia as process.

THIRD MOVEMENT

There is no permanent Code.

'Crea'

A portraiture of Gaia.
"The meaning of mystery is to be always in ambiguity". [100]

We cannot live with a traditional God and we cannot live without God. The artist encounters creation in its holiness and searches a Holy Grail for images.

"The most beautiful thing we can experience is the mysterious side of life. It is the deep feeling which is at the cradle of all true art and science. In this sense and only in this sense, I count myself amongst the most deeply religious people." [101]
[Einstein]

Are we entrusted with Aristotle words "the soul never thinks without an image?" [102]

"Art that enables us to know not by faith, but by felt experience that we are continuously there in 'paradise' is sacred." [103]

The 'paradise', the ontological, is a motion, a spectrum of molecules, not a fulfillment of time, the fulfillment of time is creation in creativity. 'Kairos' as Paul Tillich described, is the breaking in of the ultimate into a particular moment of time. [104]

In a sense, that art, that 'paradise', is all matter, is a living Kairos. The particular moment of time is in a process. The imagination makes a psychic leap. The horizon has vanished, a linear landscape has vanished. The moment of time is a moving spectacle of energy in constant change. Human species are a spontaneous bundle of bouncing cells. In a bit of irony, human comes from an ancient Indo European word, dhghem, meaning earth. It is also where our word humanity has its root. God's making man in his own image becomes, in this context, earth. God-likeness is bacteria, crawling matter of atoms. [105]

The organism of the earth, the universe, instructs the artist. The "Creator" is freed from the human image to an energy itself.

Analysis deserts mystery. Imagination prepares for the holy theater.

Quitting the realm of the human image as God is not to find a substitute or an equivalent. It is not to parallel the equivalence of God to Goddess.

The shift can be a radical affair and become the movable feast, not a permanent cornerstone for theology.

Unnamed, it is the quality of sacredness, expressed in a still life of Cezanne or a tree by Van Gogh. [106]

The patient universe is disoriented with screens multiplying a monarchy of repetitious humans in an edited popularity contest, a moving portrait of self-importance. [107]

Kandinsky had said, "The main element in art is to attempt to separate the personality from the pure and eternal." [108]

"The religious consciousness must find itself again without the aid of definite symbolism in a pure mystic immediacy. It is done with breaking up of forms." [109]

Kaufman says in his book, Theological Imagination, "The central task of theologians in every culture is to work out, to construct an image/concept of God appropriate to contemporary life." [110]

Nietzsche's Dead God is accusal motion.

To perceive the image God within the integration of all energy can set boundaries free and have God, as human in the sky, disappear.

All art is contemporary. African masks, totem poles, Greek statues, female fertility figures, Peruvian weavings, were made in their own time. The cultures' artists were in the holy now of their time, speculating upon the universe's creative meaning.

We peer from our moment in time through all time. Newton provided a canvas of the universe for Blake and Turner, and Einstein for Magritte and Rothko. Art brings to us a canvas for theology, non-institutionalized.

If our western culture is woven around the skeleton of Judeo, Christian, Islamic religions, is the breaking of the culture's skeleton a breaking of religions? [111]

Has the artist in a silent voice already entered the skeleton closet? Has the artist not been breaking a culture, but moving it from an outworn dogma into a sacred formative awareness, a compassionate non-hierarchical vision?

To see the artistry inhabit this migration from the authority of a God to the membranes of cells, is to see Redon, to see Matisse, to see Kandinsky to prowl the art galleries, and museums, to live in the membranes of the artist and encounter the intimacy of the quest.

"Theology cannot adequately understand the meaning nor satisfactorily interpret the truths of its primary sources without engaging in aesthetics." [112]

This search for an image is not a radical insight, but a critically important one, and if seriously taken has the possibility for moving the church from the outgrown God to the place where the loss of the image of God as human, Creator, Father, becomes a transforming energy for this holy planet.

If the tapestries of art were hung in the consciousness, the sacred might emerge from the linear and hierarchical. The church hymns and liturgy would not only lose exclusiveness, but the personal, humanized outworn God-Father image could lose its form. Humans would readdress themselves to earth, as species.

The artist, Redon, saw the artistic struggle as wresting meaning and beauty from raw material.

In his work, the holy stands within all matter. The pedestal is gone; linear vanishes. Flowers rest in the sky, women in clouds, hair in the sun, wings in the waters.

The world's creative spirit is in a displacement of stability. Order is disordering itself. Image is one great halo of interconnection.

The arts begin this God-ceiling removal, silently in remote artists' studios what was Cezanne saying? Cezanne imposes the sacred act of instability. The transcendent pear holds us to its own miracle; the normative takes flight into the distortion of a table tilted.

Mount St. Victoire becomes more and more abstract, losing stability. Cezanne was breaking up the orthodox. Revelation is in the stability of beauty. The God is unanchored. Chaos theory is preceding itself in image.

Nature itself is a spectrum of light, tantalizing the painter. Monet cannot hold still the earth. Einstein is knocking. Karl Barth was pulling the canvas out of reach. The theologian in a neo-orthodoxy wanted the reestablishing of authority with the "logic of obedience." [113]

But the tipling world moved on in the canvas, Matisse writes,

> "Indication of motion has meaning
> for us only if we do not isolate any
> one sensation of movement from
> preceding and from the following
> one." [114]

Matisse moves by instinct form the concrete toward the abstract, toward the general.

> "It's only that I tend toward what I
> feel, instantaneous impression
> movement was the background
> toward a kind of ecstasy." [115]

In his striving for serenity and object wholeness, was a world in a harmony. The energies of motion were like gentle ripples, like the anointing Christ in a palette.

Non descriptive, thoroughly present art was not only responding to the sociological world, but to the universe being seen as fragments, broken atoms flying in loose patterns. Music was breaking from forms, from expected rhythms.

Magritte's works are transformations of life, a world upside down.

Tillich is 'Shaking the Foundations'. Theology is pressing God into pieces while the church is still saying the Nicene Creed. God, the father, is crying into the canvases, ready for a quantum leap, the leap of faith out of the Sistine Ceiling.

Magritte's apple, held once in Christ's hand and Eve's, is floating in space. Gravity as law in a Newton's view leaves the accepted order of things. [116]

Frankenthaler's bleeding canvases are bared portrayals. One feels immersed in watery fluids, carried across the surface by gently lapping waves. The sensation of looking at a painting like <u>The Blue Head On</u>, is of actually being the drifting, floating body surrounded by and immersed in the water. The water and body as the sky are interplayed elements. [117]

Matter like a primal presence is not contained. Authority is not defined in sharp edges. Art takes us, trusts us to lose boundaries. This is not an anarchy for self-liberation, but an identity with live forms, invisible and boundless. To love thy neighbor as thyself is to love this miracle of interconnected molecules, solely responsible for our living. The cells are communal, the Eucharist moves symbol from the person Christ to the grapevine of existence. Christianity's father is unorthodox. An imagination of origin is process.

Mark Rothko had read Nietzsche's the Dionysus myth. The dismembered God falls into existence. [118]

The dismemberment of Rothko's figures was not just the Grecian sense of tragedy, but a spiritual mirroring of the disappearance of the Sistine God. The public, as does the pulpit, squirms from the breaking of icons.

The self-flattery of the church isolating a figurehead of God during the Renaissance (1600) had Giordano Bruno, a pop mystic, tied to a stake and burned alive because he declared "God is glorified not in one, but in countless suns; not in a single earth, but in thousands, I say in an infinity of worlds." [119]

From the 1940's to 1960's, Rothko's subconscious instinct like some quiet grace surfaces and becomes the luminous color planes, a cacophony of displaced energy, some torrential willingness to take the sacred into its depths.

Kandinsky stalks the cosmos and emerges with a canvas of molecular ecstasy. Yet the liturgy of the church, its dogma and theology's exegesis, remains in the rhetoric of the Sistine God and art is put in the museum.

Kandinsky in his multi colored circle represents "the dream of a world in which neither psychological nor mechanical laws appear to be valid." [120]

Scriabin in this period is saying that art is identical to religion. Schoenberg is breaking from the traditional conceptions of artistic harmony. Both he and Kandinsky are rooted in Nietzsche's philosophy. [121] Painting was the most appropriate way to communicate metaphysical messages. Kandinsky wrote that he did not believe in infallible safe forms or impeccable prescriptions. Paul Klee joins this company, reinforcing the motion of nature beyond the visual into a visceral, spiritual quality of this universe. Kandinsky's chief interest during his life was to realize "the spiritual in art." [122] His return to nature was not to the readable landscapes but to a 'natura naturans' a microcosm of organic structures belonging to the lowest form of animal life. A whole repertory of amoebic and flagellate was utilized to "celebrate a universal drama." [123]

Redon was close to Armand Clavaud, a botanist: he worked with the infinitely small, like working with the edge of the imperceptible world; that life between animal and plant, being and non being. [124]

> "Immortality is nothing but the bloom of the rate flower whose seed, he said, is at the heart of beauty: it is praise, admiration, the springing up of the divine seeds contained in a little bit of matter." [125]

The artist etches theology, the celebration is a redemption.

The Galilean revolution removed earth from the center. The 'ecozoic' period removes humans from the center and God climbs down from the sky. Incarnation is not made in flesh human, but in the community of interconnecting tissues – microbes of wonder.

Humans become species among species, not nations, races, sects, or religions isolated by caucuses or supremacies.

Paul Klee (1934) describes this reverence "the true artists are the ones who strive to approach the secret depths where the prime law fosters development and metamorphoses." [126]

> "What artist would not wish to dwell where the central factor of all, temporal and special movement what is known as the brain or heart of creation – determines all function? In the very heart of nature at the source of all creation where the secret key to all is kept." [127]

Alfred North Whitehead, Teilhard de Chardin, Mircea Eliade, lead us toward a moving creative non-human God, but stop. The baton is held in a God's hand. We search the women theologians and find a shuffling of the feminine into the same God nest. The eggs are renamed and uncovered and returned to the hand of God. The quest for the historical Jesus is historically set among women. God is re-robed in the mother robe, aprons are handed out in an exegesis of liberation.

In <u>A Big Enough God; A Feminist's Search for a Joyful Theology</u>, Sara Maitland's search ends with us back to the God-Creator. She ends her book, "There is risk, and beauty and joy. Gambling on the God who has so gambled on us does not seem too risky in the end." [128]

I eagerly read it. I had hoped to discover a woman theologian who had moved the image of God, but her theological discussion that traversed the spectrum of science, the fundamental "workings" of God, is brought back into a respectful form of what she calls the Grand Narrative, God. [129]

Like a Bultmann, she demythologized the Bible, but hardly God. Gordon Kaufman admitted, "It is hardly so obvious now that our salvation is to be found in Jesus Christ and him alone; in our day such phrases repeated too often have the ring of empty jargon." He understood that God was the central problem. "But if absolutely nothing within our experience can be directly identified as that to which term 'God" properly refers, what meaning does or can the word have?" [130] Cobb says, "Natural theology has become as never before our Christian history, a matter of utmost urgency for the church." [131]

Schubert Ogden claims "there would be little question that the end of theism (i.e. of classical theism) is indeed at hand." [132]

The end of theism is being painted. The metamorphism of the ontological is being unveiled. The ontological of theism is over.

Gibson Winter unveils theism, and images it theologically toward a liberation. His book, <u>Liberating Creation</u>, plays with the movement of our

God image as Creator, to a Gaian Process. The artistic paradigm tilts toward a dialogical, even dialectical process of creation and transformation.

Art is closest to the political theory of perpetual revelation. Gibson Winter uses this metaphor in juxtaposition to the mechanistic [authoritative] metaphor which tilts toward domination and exercises force.

"Any transformation", he says, "is diminished in the absence of art." [133] "Symbols are lived, yet they are constantly undergoing transformation of the present age." [134] "The retrieval of the creational symbolism is potentially a transformation of the present age." [135]

Vincent Ceglia, Thomas George, Margaret Johnson are painting that vision. Like Ceglia's, or a Zao-Wou-Ki's (artist, Chinese 1921-2013) paintings, this artistic vision grows out of an understanding that imagines a creator as the constellation of fluid – motion. The same holds for the "religio-ethical vision" that emerges from a liberating creative theology - philosophy. The re-symbolization of the present age can inform and empower a creative praxis. And hopefully transform a hierarchical image of humanity, to a global interconnection, that in turn, will reflect the need for environmental preservation, to a global healing. [136]

The paradigm is sliding from the ceiling from God-Creator to Gaia in process. The artist has eloped with ontology. The sacred dance is resounding, yet unnamed and always becoming.

The soul seeds itself with the fertility of an image.

To live in the ambiguity of process, to disinherit the old image, to free the homogeneric God into a biogenetic wonder, is to be in communion with Grace. Sacred is that image, profound, interconnecting, a Gaian transfusion.

Gratitude is life abundant, abundantly forming through a transformation of all existence, seen and unseen.

It is beyond words and even concepts. It is not a discovery of a new unity, but a celebration of Genesis in its deepest longing.

ENDNOTES

1.   Thomas Ketling, "The Nature of Nature", Parabola: The Magazine of Myth and Tradition, vol. XX (Spring 1995), 24.

2.   Daniel Halpern, Writers on Artists, ed. Daniel Halpern, (San Francisco: North Point Press, 1988), 106.

3,   Margaret Miles, Image as Insight: Visual Understanding in Western Christianity and Secular Culture, (Boston: Beacon Press, 1985), 16-18.

4.   Odilon Redon, To Myself: Notes on Life, Arts and Artists, Trans: Jeanne Wasserman and Mira Jacob, (New York: George Braziller, 1986), 89.

5.   Jacques Barzun, The Use and Abuse of Art, (Princeton: Bollingen Series XXXV-22, Princeton University Press, 1978), Back Cover.

6.   Ibid, 74.

7.   Ibid, 74-75.

8.   Ibid, 75.

9.   Miles, 1-14.

10.   Gerardus Van Der Leeuw, Sacred and Profane Beauty: The Holy in Art, with and introduction by Mircea Eliade, (New York: Holt Rinehart and Winston, 1963), VIII.

11.   Rudolf Otto, <u>The Idea of the Holy</u>, trans: John W. Harvey, (New York: A Galaxy Book. Oxford University Press, 1958), translator's summary.

12.   George Heyers, <u>Signs of Our Times: Theological Essays on Art in the Twentieth Century</u>, (Grand Rapids: William B. Erdman's Publications, 1980), 140.

13.   John Carey, <u>Kairos and Logos: Studies in the Roots and Implications of Paul Tillich's Theology</u>, Ed: John Carey, (United States: Mercer University Press, 1978), 4.

14.   Heyers, 140.

15.   Frank Burch Brown, <u>Religious Aesthetics</u>, (Princeton: Princeton University Press, 1989), 84.

16.   Ibid, 84.

17.   Ibid, 193.

18.   Ibid. 193.

19.   Herbert Reed, <u>Contemporary British Art</u>, (Middlesex, Great Britain: Penguin Books, Harmondsworth, 1951), 36.

20.   Fritjof Capra, <u>Turning Point Science, Society and the Rising Culture</u>, (New York: Simon and Schuster, 1982), 39-48.

21.   Fritjof Capra, <u>Uncommon Wisdom:</u>
<u>Conversations with Remarkable People,</u> (New York:
Simon and Schuster, 1988), 51.

22.   Paul Corby Finney, <u>The Invisible God: The</u>
<u>Earliest Christian Art</u>, (New York: Oxford Press,
1994).

23.   David E. Martin, <u>Art and the Religious</u>
<u>Experience: The Language of the Sacred</u>, (Cranberry,
New Jersey: Associated University Press, Bucknell
University Press, 1972), 53.

24.   Martin, 68.

25.   Thomas Berry, Lecture at Union Theological
Seminary, Pierre Teilhard De Chardin Lecture, Fall
1994.

26.   Miles, 1.

27.   John Berger, <u>Ways of Seeing</u>, (London: British
Broadcasting Corporation and Penguin Books, 1972),
7.

28.   Ibid, 7.

29.   Gordon D. Kaufman, <u>The Theological</u>
<u>Imagination: Constructing the Concept of God,</u>
(Philadelphia: Westminster Press, 1981), 10.

30.   Berger, 10.

31. Louis Baldwin, <u>Portraits of God</u>, (Jefferson, North Carolina: McFarland and Company, 1986), 9-10.

32. Gerda Lerner, <u>The Creation of Patriarchy</u>, (New York: Oxford University Press, 1986) 7-14.

33. Raimon Panikkar, <u>Myth, Faith and Hermeneutics</u>, (New York: Paulist Press, 1979), 90.

34. Nicholas Gier, <u>Philosophy East and West: A Quarterly of Comparative Philosophy</u>, (University of Hawaii Press, January 25, 1995), 90.

35. Baldwin, 26.

36. Gier, 74.

37. Erich Neumann, <u>Art and the Unconscious</u>, (Princeton: Bollingen Series LXI, Princeton University Press, 1959) 86.

38. Martin, 24.

39. Neumann, 88.

40. Van Der Leeuw, 157.

41. Ibid, 162-163.

42. Ibid, 164.

43. Visser T. Hooft, <u>Rembrandt and the Gospel</u>, (New York: Living Age Books, Meridian Books, 1960), 33.

44.   Ernst Cassirer, <u>The Philosophy of Symbolic Forms: Mythological Thought Vol. II</u>, (New Haven: Yale University Press, 1955), 218.

45.   Finney, IX.

46.   Ketling, 27.

47.   Miles, 43-46.

48.   Finney, 100 and 150.

49.   Miles, 142.

50.   Finney, 42.

51.   Miles, 95.

52.   Finney, 43.

53.   Miles, 48.

54.   Ibid, 43.

55.   Ibid, 44.

56.   Finney, 58.

57.   Ibid, 69.

58.   Ibid, 86.

59.   Miles, 96.

60.   Ibid, 96.

61.　Ibid, 97.

62.　Ibid, 99.

63.　Ibid, 107.

64.　Ibid, 143.

65.　Brown, 84.

66.　Henry K. Skolimowski, <u>Eco Theology: Toward a Religion for Our Times</u>, (Adyar, Madras. India: Vasanta Press, 1985), 312.

67.　Brown, 91.

68.　Ibid, 91.

69.　Anthony Burgess, <u>Flame of Being</u>, (London: William Heinemann Ltd, 1985), XI.

70.　Miles, 140.

71.　Ibid, 140.

72.　Ibid, 135.

73.　Scot McVay, conversation, 1995.

74.　E. H. Ramsden, <u>The Letters of Michelangelo, Vol. I</u>, Ed: E. H. Ramsden, (San Francisco: Stanford University Press, 1963), 19.

75.　Van Der Leeuw, 180.

76. Ibid, 335-336.

77. Ramsden, 19.

78. Ibid, 20.

79. Ibid, 21.

80. Ramsden, Vol. 2, XVII.

81. Ibid, LII.

82. Ibid, LII.

83. David Summers, Michelangelo and the Language of Art, (Princeton: Princeton University Press, 1941), 14.

84. Ibid, 14.

85. Ibid, 14.

86. Ibid, 17.

87. Ibid, 19.

88. Ibid, 3.

89. Sallie McFague, Models for God: Theology for an Ecological Nuclear Age, (Philadelphia: Fortress Press, 1987), 81.

90. Kaufman, 10.

91. McFague, 81.

92.   Kaufman, 275.

93.   Paul Tillich, <u>The Religious Situation</u>, (New York: Meridian Books, 1956), 85.

94.   Richard Elliott Friedman, <u>The Disappearance of God: A Divine Mystery</u>, (New York: Little Brown and Company, 1995), 118.

95.   Ibid, 129.

96.   Timothy Ferris, <u>Coming of Age in the Milky Way</u>, (New York: William Morrow, 1988), 203.

97.   Ibid, 227.

98.   Lynn Margules and Dorian Sagan, <u>Microcosmos: Four Billion Years of Microbial Evolution, forward by Dr. Lewis Clark</u>, (New York: Simon and Schuster, 1988), 14.

99.   Ibid, 27.

100. Redon, 89.

101. Martin, 25.

102. Rudolf Arnheim, Visual Thinking, (Berkeley: University of California Press, 1969), 12.

103.   Rollo May, The Courage to Create, (New York: W. W. Norton and Company, 1975), 42.

104.   Paul Tillich, <u>On Art and Architecture</u>, Ed: John Dillenberger and Jane Dillenberger, (New York: Crossroad, 1989), 184.

105.   Margules, 14.

106.   Tillich, <u>The Religious Situation</u>, 89.

107.   The patient universe is disoriented with video and television and computer screens, multiplying a monarchy of human in a repetitious edited popularity contest; a moving portrait of self-importance.

108.   Jacques Maritain, <u>Creative Intuition in Art</u>, (New York: Bollingen Series, IIIVI, Pantheon Books, 1953), 217.

109.   Tillich, <u>The Religious Situation</u>, 89.

110.   Kaufman, 279.

111.   Skolimowski, 44.

112.   Brown, 44.

113.   Mary Jean Irion, <u>From the Ashes of Christianity</u>, (Philadelphia: J. B. Lippincott and Co., 1968), 130.

114.   H. Barr Jr., <u>Matisse: His Art and his Public</u>, (New York: Museum of Modern Art, 1940), 120.

115.   Ibid, 160.

116.   David Sylvester, <u>The Silence of the World,</u> (New York: Henry Abrams, The Menil Foundation, 1992), 110.

117.   Barbara Rose, <u>Frankenthaler</u>, (New York: Henry Abrams, 1969), 80.

118.   Bonnie Clearwater, <u>Mark Rothko Works on Paper</u>, (New York: Hudson Hills Press, 1979), 25.

119.   Ferris, 370.

120.   Hans K. Roebel with Jean K. Benjamin, <u>Kandinsky</u>, (New York: Hudson Hills Press, 1979), 120.

121.   Ibid, 19.

122.   Ibid, 42.

123.   Ibid, 42.

124.   Redon, 14.

125.   Ibid, 122.

126.   Gualtieri Di San Lazzaro, <u>Klee</u>, (New York: Frederick Praeger, 1957), 142.

127.   Ibid, 142.

128.   Sara Maitland, <u>A Big Enough God: A Feminist Search for a Joyful Theology</u>, (New York: Henry Hill and Co., 1995), 190.

129. Ibid

130. Irion, 57.

131. Ibid, 40.

132. Ibid, 132.

133. Gibson Winter, <u>Liberating Creation: Foundations of Religious Social Ethics</u>, (New York: Crossroads, 1981), 128.

134. Ibid, 125.

135. Ibid, 115.

136. Ibid, 115.

Rev. Margo E. Fish

Margo E. Fish, B.A., A.A. (Fine Arts), M.Div. Margo Fish graduated from Union Theological Seminary ('96), is the mother of four children and was married to theologian Howard (Mac) Fish. She is an artist and poet and religion teacher living in New York City and the Adirondack Mountains. She has had over twenty one-person shows of her painting in the United States and has shown at the Edinburgh Festival in Scotland, Oxford University, Princeton University, Hydra, Greece, and most recently at Lake Placid Center for the Arts. Her paintings are in private collections in Europe and in North American. In 2014 she illustrated "The Poetry of the Rev. Dr. James A. Forbes."

Margo and her husband purchased a cabin on Lake Placid in New York in 1957. During their summers, she and Mac hand-built 15 separate living structures on the property--a kitchen, dining room, chapel, study, sleeping cabins for visitors, a salon for evening entertainments, and much more. The property is named "Tapawingo" and has been featured recently in Adirondack Life Magazine and other publications, including the New York Times. Concerts, plays, and poetry readings are presented in the salon during the summer. Tapawingo is only accessible by footpath or boat. Margo has also run 50 marathons, and was one of the first women to run in the 1967 Boston Marathon.

In conjunction with art and theology, she organized
women from all faiths to conserve an ancient
monument on the Isle of Iona, Scotland.